World of Wonder

OCEAN LIFE

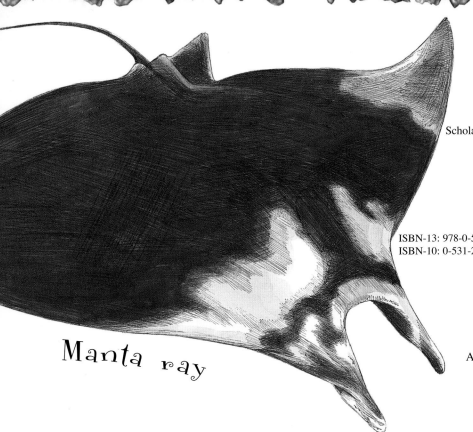

Manta ray

The nautilus has a large head
with up to 90 tentacles. It lives in
a shell and swims by squirting
water out through its siphon.

Eye

Tentacles

Siphon

Published in Great Britain in 2008 by
The Salariya Book Company Ltd
25 Marlborough Place, Brighton BN1 1UB

ISBN-13: 978-0-531-20451-1 (lib. bdg.)   978-0-531-20542-6 (pbk.)
ISBN-10: 0-531-20451-0 (lib. bdg.)   0-531-20542-8 (pbk.)

Author and artist: Carolyn Franklin is
a graduate of Brighton College of Art,
England, specializing in design and
illustration. She has worked in animation
and advertising, and has written and
illustrated many natural-history books
for children.

Consultant: Peter Jones is a Research
Curator with an advanced degree in
animal science.

Editor: Stephen Haynes

PAPER FROM

SUSTAINABLE FORESTS

World of Wonder
Ocean Life

Written and illustrated by

Carolyn Franklin

children's press®

An Imprint of Scholastic Inc.

NEW YORK • TORONTO • LONDON • AUCKLAND • SYDNEY

MEXICO CITY • NEW DELHI • HONG KONG

DANBURY, CONNECTICUT

Contents

What Lives in the Ocean?

The ocean is huge—it covers nearly seven tenths of the earth's surface. Polar oceans are cold, tropical oceans are warm, and some inland seas are very salty. From shallow coastal waters to great ocean depths, the ocean supports a vast number of different plants and animals.

Animals called **vertebrates**, such as fish, whales, seals, turtles, and penguins, live in the ocean. So do the weird and wonderful **invertebrates**, such as crabs, lobsters, jellyfish, squids, octopuses, sea urchins, starfish, and corals.

What Lives in the Sand and Mud?

Most of the animals that live on sandy and muddy shores live in burrows beneath the surface. Cockles, clams, and lugworms all remain hidden even when the tide has risen, using tiny tubes or siphons to feed.

The hard clam uses its "foot" to bury itself in the sand. When the tide comes in, it sticks two tubes up through the sand. With one it sucks in seawater and food, and with the other it gets rid of any waste.

True or False?

A mouse can live in the sand and mud. **?**

Answers on page 31

Amphitrite

Soft-shell clam

Hard clam

Some crabs feed on the surface, retreating to the safety of their burrows when the tide goes out.

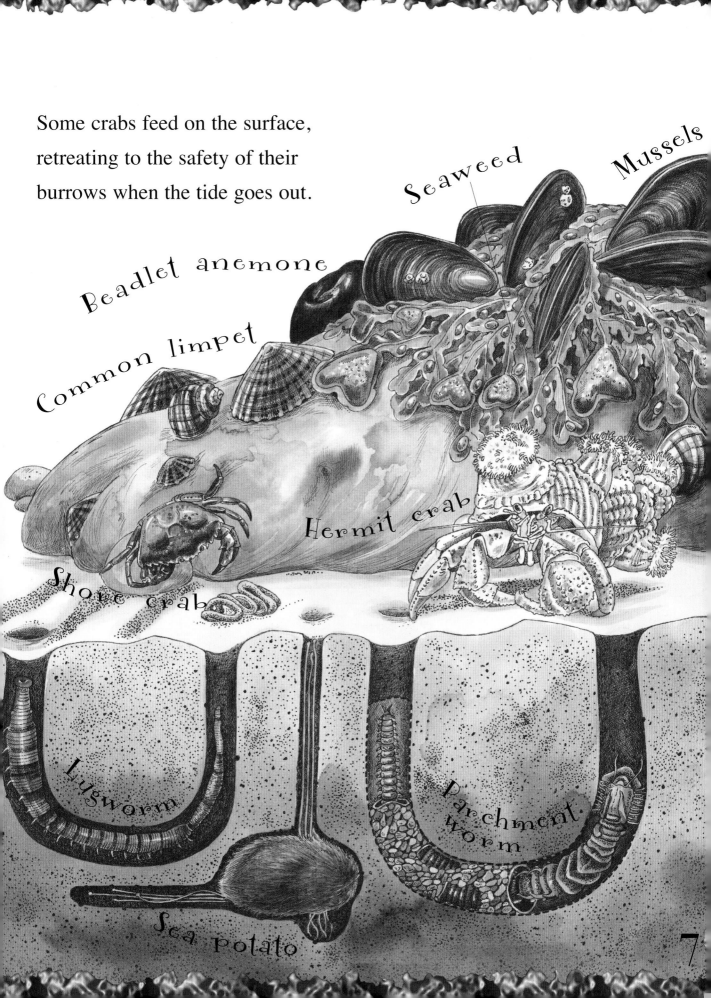

Seaweed

Mussels

Beadlet anemone

Common limpet

Hermit crab

Shore crab

Lugworm

Parchment worm

Sea potato

What Lives on the Rocks?

Teeming with life, rock pools provide shelter for many animals. Barnacles, limpets, sea anemones and seaweeds grip the rocks tightly. At high tide the mussels open their shells to feed.

Seaweed

Common limpet

Whelk shell with anemones

Hermit crab

A starfish pulls apart the shell of a mussel, then digests the flesh of the mussel inside.

Starfish

Mussels

Beadlet anemone

Edible crab

Shore crab

What Lives Near the Surface of the Ocean?

Sunlight enables plants, mostly **algae**, to grow at depths of more than 300 feet. Tiny animals live among the algae. These very small plants and animals, called **plankton**, drift in the seas, pulled along by tides and currents. Flying fish, sardines, whale sharks, and huge **filter-feeding** whales eat the plankton. Smaller fish like herrings and anchovies are eaten by larger fish, seals, dolphins, and birds.

True or False?

Jellyfish eat fish and are full of water.

Answers on page 31

How clever!

Dolphins live together in groups called **pods.** They eat mainly fish and squid. Dolphins are very intelligent, each making its own special whistles and clicks underwater. The Atlantic dolphin can dive down to 1,000 feet and jump 20 feet out of the water.

Black-headed gull

Dolphins

Flying fish

Violet jellyfish

School of mackerel

Tuna

Marlin

Ocean sunfish

The ocean sunfish is the heaviest bony fish in the world. It can weigh up to 5,000 pounds.

11

What Lives on the Ocean Floor?

Near to land the ocean floor is shallow; it is covered with mud, sand, and small stones. Attached to the rocks live sponges, corals, barnacles, and sea squirts. Far from land the ocean floor can be very deep, with underwater mountains, valleys, and trenches.

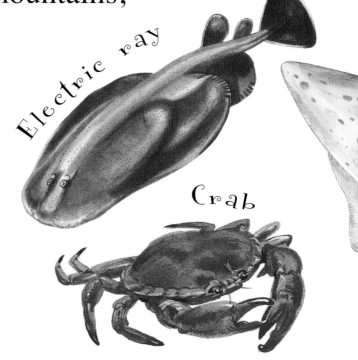

Lobster

Electric ray

Crab

Crabs, lobsters, shrimp, starfish, sea urchins, and marine snails crawl along the bottom searching for food.

True or False?

Octopuses have two hearts and can hear well underwater.

? ? ?

Answers on page 31

Octopus

Most octopuses live in dens on the ocean floor. They hunt mainly at night. They use their arms to catch prey, then kill it by biting it with their tough beak. Poison softens the prey's flesh and the octopus sucks it out.

Siphon

Arm

Suckers

Squid

Tentacle

Like octopuses, squids eat all kinds of sea creatures, from tiny shrimps, lobsters, limpets, and worms, to huge fish. They even eat other squids and octopuses. The Atlantic giant squid grows up to 60 feet long.

13

What Lives in the Deep?

Below 300 feet there is little or no sunlight and it is very cold. No plants can survive. Many animals live on food that falls down from above. Others swim up to the light to find food. Below 2,000 feet there is extreme pressure from the weight of the freezing-cold, pitch-black water above.

Gulper

Deep-sea squid

Deep-sea hatchetfish

Deep-sea prawn

Scaly dragonfish

True or False?

A fish can make light.

? ? ? ? ?

Answers on page 31

Huge jaws!

Food is scarce in the ocean depths and most deep-sea fish are small. Many, like the hatchetfish, are specially adapted with huge, powerful jaws and long, sharp teeth. Others, such as the gulper, have a massive mouth so that they can swallow animals larger than themselves.

What Is a Coral Reef?

A coral reef is formed from the stony skeletons of tiny animals called **coral polyps**. Algae live on the polyps, as do sponges, anemones, and clams. Animals feed on the coral or use it as a home.

Green parrotfish

Blacktip reef shark

Crown of thorns starfish

Elkhorn coral

Blue-striped grunts

Parrotfish

There are many wonderful types, sizes, and colors of coral, and not all of them make reefs. Parrotfish eat the algae that grow on rocks and coral. They scrape off the algae with their hard, beak-like mouths.

Moray eel

Moray eels live hidden in the corals or among rocks in warm, tropical seas. Most moray eels hunt at night. They eat mainly fish, as well as octopuses, lobsters, and other eels.

Trumpetfish

Soft coral

Hawksbill turtle

Queen angelfish

Sea fan coral

Tubeworms

What Fish Live in the Ocean?

Fish use **gills** to breathe underwater. Most fish are streamlined and have **fins** to help them balance and steer. Sharks, sailfish, swordfish, and tuna are fast hunters. Some fish live by themselves, while others live in huge schools.

Puffer fish

When frightened, puffer fish puff themselves up with air. Once puffed up, their spines stand out and they become harder for other fish to eat.

Harlequin tusk fish

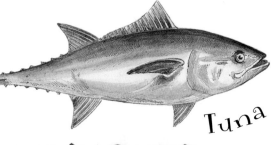

Tuna

Leafy sea dragon

Looking like a piece of floating seaweed, the leafy sea dragon is hard to spot. It creeps up on small shrimp, then uses its long, thin snout to suck them into its mouth.

Conger eel

Scorpion fish

True or False?

Some fish have wings and can fly.

? ? ? ?

Answers on page 31

Lemon sole

What Mammals Live in the Ocean?

Porpoise

Killer whale

Mammals that live in the sea have to return to the surface for air. Seals, sea lions, and walruses are furry sea mammals. The smallest sea mammal is the sea otter; the largest is the blue whale. Dolphins, porpoises, and other **toothed whales** are mammals. Dugongs and manatees are sea mammals that eat only plants, mainly grasses.

Dugong and young

A dugong uses its tail and short forelimbs to move about. Its snout points downward to help it graze.

Grey whale

Baleen plates

Grey whales can grow up to 50 feet long and weigh 38 tons. Despite their size, they eat mainly tiny invertebrates from the ocean floor. They suck up mouthfuls of mud and strain it through their **baleen** plates.

True or False?
A **walrus** uses its **tusks** to dig for food.

Answers on page 31

Walrus

Do Birds Live in the Ocean?

No, birds don't live in the ocean, but many types of birds depend on the ocean for their food. Some, like albatrosses, penguins, and auks, spend nearly all their life out at sea. Penguins are the best adapted of all the sea birds. They have flippers instead of wings and can swim and dive for food.

Puffin

True or False?

A **puffin** can carry up to 30 fish in its beak.

Answers on page 31

Puffins and guillemots are birds that can rest on the water.

Herring gulls

Gulls, terns, and sea ducks feed in the seas close to land. Other birds, such as cormorants and shags, dive down from the surface to hunt for fish. When the tide goes out, wading birds search for food along the exposed shore.

Edible crab

Albatross

The wandering albatross has the largest wingspan of any bird, up to 10 feet. Albatrosses spend most of their time flying over the oceans, returning to land only to breed.

What Is a Food Chain?

A food chain shows how each living thing, from large to small, gets its food.

Great white shark

Grey reef shark

Marlin

Baleen whale

All living things depend on each other to live. Some animals eat plants, and some eat other animals. All sea creatures rely on other sea creatures for food. At the bottom of the food chain are the sea plants and plankton.

24

Answers on page 31

True or False?

A blue whale will eat up to 7,900 pounds of animal plankton a day.

?

Ocean sunfish

Tuna

Lancet fish

Barracuda

Lantern fish

Animal plankton

The plankton that floats near the surface is eaten by slightly larger creatures that are then eaten by tiny fish. The tiny fish are eaten by larger fish, and these are finally eaten by even bigger creatures such as killer whales and sharks.

Dead plankton falls to the ocean floor and feeds the creatures that live there.

Plant plankton

25

What Lives Under the Ice?

At the north and south poles the ocean is very cold and salty. The only plants there are plant plankton, which is eaten by tiny shrimp called krill.

True or False?

Killer whales eat krill.

Answers on page 31

Chinstrap penguins

Penguins live only in the southern hemisphere. These Chinstrap penguins have one or two chicks each summer, which they fight to protect. They live and breed in large groups, mainly eating fish and krill.

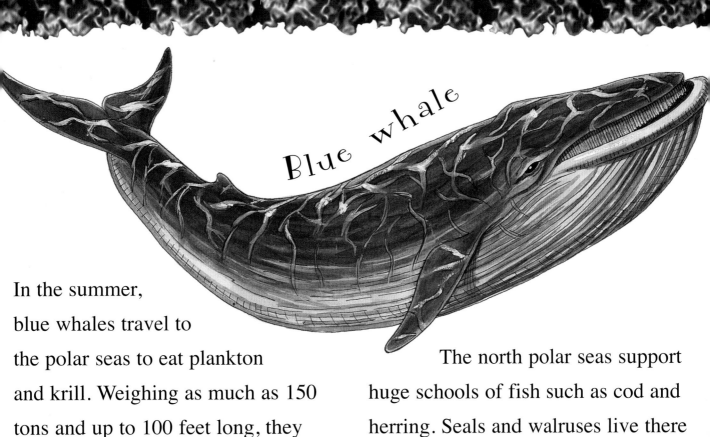

Blue whale

In the summer,
blue whales travel to
the polar seas to eat plankton
and krill. Weighing as much as 150
tons and up to 100 feet long, they
are the largest animals that have
ever lived on Earth.

The north polar seas support
huge schools of fish such as cod and
herring. Seals and walruses live there
all year round. Killer whales are found
in all seas, but mostly in the Antarctic.

Antarctic petrel

Weddell seals

Killer whale

Adélie penguins

Emperor penguins

What Is Migration?

Many sea creatures make regular journeys at certain times of the year, either to find food or to breed; this is called migration. Turtles, penguins, and seals all migrate long distances from the ocean to lay eggs or give birth on land.

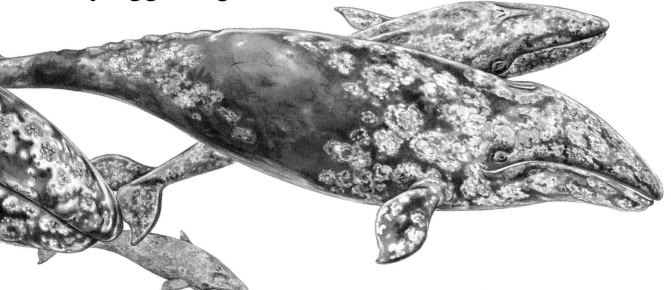

Grey whales

Grey whales make one of the longest migrations of any mammal. Each year they travel from the Arctic Ocean to Mexico and back again, a distance of up to 14,000 miles.

European and American eels travel up to 3,000 miles across the Atlantic Ocean. Salmon return to breed in the streams where they hatched, and can swim long distances upstream.

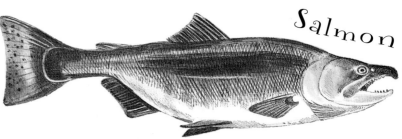

Salmon

Sea turtles lay their eggs on land. Many lose their special nesting grounds when hotels and houses are built on them.

Green turtle

What Problems Do Oceans Face?

Our seas and oceans are in danger. Oil from huge tankers and waste from factories and cities are killing sea creatures and damaging coral reefs.

Overfishing by man results in the number of fish in the sea getting smaller. Some sea animals are hit by boats. Others get trapped in fishing nets.

Hooded seal pup covered in oil

Oil and trash

Useful Words

Giant squid

Coelacanth

Algae Simple plants with no roots, flowers, or leaves. Algae live in wet places and include seaweeds.

Baleen Stiff plates inside the mouth of some whales, used to filter krill and plankton from water.

Coral polyp A small, soft-bodied invertebrate animal with a hard, stony outside. This animal lives mainly in large groups or colonies.

Filter-feeder An animal that feeds by filtering its food from water.

Fins Used by most fish to help them move through water.

Gills Used by fish to breathe underwater.

Invertebrate An animal without a backbone.

Mammal A warm-blooded animal with hair or fur, which feeds its young on milk.

Plankton Tiny plants and animals that float and drift in the sunlit waters of the sea.

Pod A family group of whales or other sea mammals.

Prey A creature hunted for food.

Toothed whale A whale with teeth instead of baleen plates.

Vertebrate An animal with a backbone.

Answers

Page 6 **TRUE!** A small hairy worm called a sea mouse lives in the sand. It eats other worms up to three times its own length.

Page 10 **TRUE!** Jellyfish are made from up to 98% water. Found in every ocean, they catch fish to eat in their long tentacles.

Page 12 **FALSE!** An octopus has three hearts. One heart pumps blood through the body and the other two pump blood through its gills. Octopuses are unable to hear.

Page 15 **TRUE!** Many deep-sea fish make their own light. The deep-sea anglerfish uses a luminous lure above its huge mouth to attract prey.

Page 19 **FALSE!** Fish cannot fly. However, there are some amazing fish *called* flying fish. They have long, thin fins which they use to glide short distances above the surface of the water.

Page 21 **FALSE!** Walruses use their snouts to dig for food on the muddy sea floor. They use their long tusks to make holes in the polar ice so that they can find food. Males also use their tusks for fighting.

Page 22 **TRUE!** A puffin can catch up to 30 small fish and carry them in its beak to feed its young.

Page 25 **TRUE!** Blue whales dive down as deep as 300 feet, taking a huge mouthful of plankton-rich seawater as they go. The water is then squeezed out through the baleen plates. Once its mouth is clear of water, the whale swallows the plankton that is left behind.

Page 26 **FALSE!** Killer whales—or orcas, as they are also called—eat fish and other sea mammals such as seals, sea lions, and even larger whales.

Hammerhead shark

Index

(Illustrations are shown in **bold type**.)

Clownfish

Parrotfish eating algae on coral